Train Trivia

Railroad & Train
Multiple Choice
Questions & Answers

200 Train & Railroad Themed Multiple Choice Questions!

Train & Railroad Trivia
Questions

#1. Internationally called railways, which country calls them railroads instead?
a) Peru
b) the U.S.A.
c) Great Britain
d) Norway

#2. The term "high ball" refers to an early type of:
a) American signaling system
b) railroad tie
c) bench seat
d) locomotive engine

#3. In 1865, a funeral train carried Abraham Lincoln's body through how many American cities?
a) 70
b) 95
c) 180
d) 125

#4. In what year was the first steam locomotive invented?
a) 1800
b) 1829
c) 1804
d) 1902

#5. A train trip organized by this person in 1841 was the beginning of the first travel agency...
a) George Bush
b) Thomas Cook
c) Christopher Columbus
d) Jim Quinn

#6. Robbie Robertson tells you to catch this train in his song "Somewhere Down the Crazy River"...
a) Ghost Train
b) The Blue Train
c) Northbound Train
d) The Crazy Train

#7. What train is known as crazy eights?
a) a runaway train
b) a high-speed train
c) an unbalanced train
d) a train on the wrong route

#8. A train trip from Portugal to Vietnam is the longest in the world, at 10, 056 miles. How long does this trip take?
a) 12 days
b) 21 days
c) 16 days
d) 10 days

#9. In what country did the Great Train Robbery occur?
a) the U.S.A.
b) Spain
c) Great Britain
d) Austria

#10. What gang from Indiana operated mainly in the American midwest?
a) Bummers Gang
b) Doolin-Dalton Gang
c) James Gang
d) Reno Gang

#11. How much of the world's cargo is transported by train?
a) 35%
b) 65%
c) 40%
d) 50%

#12. This vast railway network connects much of Russia:
a) The Orient Express
b) Trans-Siberian Express
c) The Sweet Train
d) The Glacier Express

#13. What board game allows you to buy & sell railroads?
a) Risk
b) Sorry
c) Monopoly
d) Clue

#14. The Stockton & Darlington in Great Britain was the first one of these in the world:
a) underground railroad
b) public railroad
c) private railroad
d) Royal railroad

#15. What country did not have an established railroad by 1840?
a) Mongolia
b) France
c) Austria
d) Germany

#16. The song "City of New Orleans" describes a train ride from:
a) Boston to New Orleans
b) New Orleans to Philadelphia
c) Kansas City to New Orleans
d) Chicago to New Orleans

#17. How long have railroads been in continuous operation in the U.S.A.?
a) almost 100 years
b) almost 250 years
c) almost 400 years
d) almost 200 years

#18. What are the names of the first two models of Pullman cars?
a) the Pioneer & the Springfield
b) the Pioneer & the Tornado
c) the Sweet Seat & the Springwater
d) the Lincoln & the Pullman Palace

#19. Modern bullet trains can reach speeds of more than:
a) 250 miles per hour
b) 125 miles per hour
c) 425 miles per hour
d) 300 miles per hour

#20. The 1971 song by Cat Stevens was titled:
a) Love Train
b) Fast Train
c) Peace Train
d) Harmony Train

#21. When were diesel trains introduced in the U.S.A.?
a) 1940's
b) 1920's
c) 1890's
d) 1950's

#22. "20th Century Limited" was a famous express passenger train that ran between these two cities from 1902 until 1967:
a) Denver & New Orleans
b) New York & Chicago
c) Miami & New York
d) Chicago & Buffalo

#23. The 1980 heavy metal song "Crazy Train" was released by
a) The Scorpions
b) Van Halen
c) Ozzy Osbourne
d) Ronnie James Dio

#24. What year did the Reno Gang commit the first peacetime train robbery?
a) 1870
b) 1881
c) 1866
d) 1902

#25. What travels on the "Spanish Train" in Chris de Burgh's song?
a) exotic animals
b) mail
c) souls of the dead
d) circus performers

#26. The majority of history's train robberies occurred in this country:
a) Canada
b) the U.S.A.
c) Mexico
d) Brazil

#27. The Orient Express was the scene for a murder detective novel by this author:
a) Harper Lee
b) Amy Tan
c) Margaret Atwood
d) Agatha Christie

#28. Which is not a real, luxury train name?
a) Rocky Express
b) The Ghan
c) Indian Pacific
d) The Canadian

#29. Who was responsible for the 1899 Wilcox Train Robbery?
a) Bill Downing
b) Jesse James
c) Butch Cassidy & the Wild Bunch
d) Frank James

#30. What color were Russian First Class trains painted?
a) brown
b) gray
c) blue
d) black

#31. Where would you find the train called The Flying Hamburger in the 1930s?
a) Scotland
b) Germany
c) Spain
d) Italy

#32. Led Zeppelin sang about being on a train in this song:
a) Black Dog
b) Ramble On
c) Stairway to Heaven
d) Bring it on Home

#33. London, England built the first subterranean railroad in the world, later known as "the Underground", in this year:
a) 1884
b) 1902
c) 1908
d) 1863

#34. Many years after England, this city built the second subterranean railroad in the world:
a) Budapest, Hungary
b) Paris, France
c) Tokyo, Japan
d) Luxemburg, Germany

#35. What was the outcome of a race between a horse and the first steam locomotive?
a) the horse won
b) the train crashed
c) the train won
d) the horse died

#36. The first steam locomotive in America was imported from England. When did they build their first train?
a) later the same year
b) the following year
c) two years later
d) five years later

#37. This is an Alfred Hitchcock movie from 1951:
a) Murder on the Orient Express
b) Training Day
c) Unstoppable
d) Strangers on a Train

#38. What number appears on the side of the fictional steam train Thomas the Tank Engine?
a) 1
b) 101
c) 515
d) 5

#39. What year was the Great Train Robbery?
a) 1949
b) 1971
c) 1955
d) 1963

#40. How many miles of train tracks were laid in the U.S.A. by 1850?
a) 6500 miles
b) 4000 miles
c) 9000 miles
d) 1000 miles

#41. The original route for this train between Paris and Istanbul (then Constantinople) operated between 1883 & 1977:
a) Blue Train
b) Orient Express
c) Golden Arrow
d) Glacier Express

#42. What 1987 train comedy was inspired by the 1951 movie "Strangers on a Train"?
a) City Slickers
b) The Cannonball Run
c) Planes, Trains and Automobiles
d) Throw Momma from the Train

#43. An image of the earliest known wooden tracks used for transportation in Germany goes back to this date, well before trains were invented:
a) 1425
b) 1705
c) 1575
d) 1350

#44. Train transportation made it possible for the U.S.A. to end this:
a) plantations
b) feudalism
c) socialism
d) the Civil War

#45. What was the first railroad line in the U.S.A.?
a) Baltimore & Ohio Railroad
b) Pennsylvania Railroad
c) Illinois Central Railroad
d) Central Pacific Railroad

#46. What is the job title of the driver of the train?
a) Engineer
b) Conductor
c) Brakeman
d) Coach Attendant

#47. Who operates the horn on an American train?
a) Engineer
b) Conductor
c) Brakeman
d) Coach Attendant

#48. The song "King of the Road" is about:
a) being a train passenger
b) riding the rails
c) a train robbery
d) being an Engineer

#49. In what country will you find the Blue Train?
a) England
b) India
c) Africa
d) Vietnam

#50. Who stole the greatest sum from an American train robbery?
a) Butch Cassidy & the Wild Bunch
b) the Dalton Gang
c) Jesse James
d) Newton Gang

#51. The Monkees sang about the Last Train to this place:
a) Liverpool
b) London
c) Buffalo
d) Clarksville

#52. In the mid-19th century, railroads and banks were the momentum behind:
a) entrepreneurship
b) socialism
c) capitalism
d) debt

#53. What is the name of the train in Harry Potter?
a) Hogsmeade Express
b) The Hogwarts Express
c) The Hogwarts Bullet
d) King's Cross Express

#54. How did most train robbers get on the train?
a) boarded like other passengers
b) horseback
c) dropped by airplane
d) hiding on the roof

#55. Where is Grand Central Station located?
a) Chicago
b) Atlanta
c) New York
d) Los Angeles

#56. What is railroad gauge?
a) the angle tracks are laid
b) the width of the crossties
c) the width between two rails
d) the thickness of one rail

#57.1970s Canadian band the Stampeders had a hit with the song "Monday Morning Choo Choo" as well as this train song:
a) I'll Be There
b) Sweet City Woman
c) September
d) Sweet Baby James

#58. What happened to William Huskisson at the opening of the first railroad?
a) he got married afterward
b) he fell off the train
c) he was fatally wounded by a train
d) he broke his leg

#59. What is a berth on a train?
a) storage compartment
b) engine
c) sleeping compartment
d) nursery

#60. Which is not a job for the Conductor in the U.S.A.?
a) record keeping
b) ticket collection
c) operating the horn
d) staying on schedule

#61. The earliest tracks used wagons to haul:
a) large animals
b) heavy loads from the mines
c) large rocks from the land
d) groups of workmen

#62. Who was "the father of railroads" in America?
a) Henry Ford
b) George Stephenson
c) Denis Papin
d) Marc Seguin

#63. Gladys Knight and the Pips sang this 1970s train-themed hit:
a) Soul Train
b) Midnight Train to Georgia
c) Chatanooga Choo Choo
d) Love Train

#64. Where will you find a cupola?
a) railroad track
b) locomotive
c) passenger car
d) caboose

#65. Railroads made it necessary to standardize this internationally:
a) language
b) train size
c) time
d) currency

#66. The first rails, found in Germany for a mining cart, were made from this material:
a) iron
b) steel
c) limestone
d) wood

#67. The following is not a real train-sounding musical act:
a) Grand Funk Railroad
b) Railroad Jones
c) Boxcar Willie
d) Train

#68. What is the technology behind maglev trains?
a) solar power
b) nuclear power
c) magnetic force
d) quantum physics

#69. Which of the following is not a real train signal system:
a) semaphore signal
b) double disc signal
c) ball signal
d) chain signal

#70. In what country will you find the Glacier Express route?
a) Switzerland
b) Austria
c) Canada
d) Russia

#71. The year 1891 saw the first mass-marketed model train sets in this country:
a) China
b) the U.S.A.
c) Germany
d) England

#72. The name of the platform for the locomotive driver is:
a) Step plate
b) Footplate
c) Alcove
d) Cupola

#73. This train robber was a member of the gang from the "Great Train Robbery", who got away, for a few years...
a) Frank James
b) Butch Cassidy
c) Buster Edwards
d) Ronnie Biggs

#74. In what country will you find 478 km of absolutely straight railway tracks, the longest stretch in the world?
a) Canada
b) Brazil
c) Australia
d) Africa

#75. Canada's only two train robberies were committed by Bill Miner, also:
a) a banker
b) an American
c) a police officer
d) a miner

#76. By 1916, the U.S.A. had a quarter of a million miles of railways. Approximately how many do they have today?
a) 430, 000 miles
b) 1 million miles
c) 170, 000 miles
d) 3 million miles

#77. Cuba was the first Latin American country to build railroads to transport this, not for local transportation:
a) tobacco
b) livestock
c) sugar
d) tourists

#78. The "Settebello" luxury train in Italy has these at both the front and rear of the train:
a) observation lounges
b) casinos
c) restaurants
d) day spas

#79. Famous basketball player LeBron James appeared in this 2015 film:
a) Ghost Train
b) 3:10 to Yuma
c) Trainwreck
d) Switchback

#80. This happened in 1971 to railroads in Greece:
a) switched to electric
b) doubled in size
c) became obsolete
d) became state owned

#81. In celebration of an east-west link, the Union Pacific and Central Pacific Railroads did this:
a) the last spike is hand carved
b) the railroad ties are steel
c) the last spike is gold
d) the rails are gold

#82. The joining of the American east and west by rail is sometimes called the:
a) railway wedding
b) united junction
c) American honeymoon
d) Pacific powerhouse

#83. What is the most popular engine type in use today in the U.S.A.?
a) electric
b) diesel
c) coal
d) natural gas

#84. Which American President had a special armored train car made called the Ferdinand Magellan?
a) Harry Truman
b) Franklin Roosevelt
c) Lyndon Johnson
d) Dwight Eisenhower

#85. Railroads are responsible for the creation of this time routine:
a) 9-5
b) 8-4
c) 7-3
d) 10-6

#86. The British steam locomotive "Mallard" reached a record-setting speed of 126 mph in 1938. Since then:
a) many steam engines have broken this record
b) the train derailed at high speed
c) Mallard is still in daily use
d) no steam engine has broken this record

#87. Which is not a real Canadian railroad?
a) Alberta Bound
b) Canadian Pacific
c) Via-Rail
d) Ontario Northland

#88. Sam Smith sings about this type of train:
a) Train Wreck
b) Last Train Home
c) Midnight Train
d) Downtown Train

#89. What is the front car of a train called?
a) locomotive
b) caboose
c) cabin
d) carriage

#90. In the U.S.A., what is the legal limit on the length of a freight train?
a) 100 cars
b) no legal limit exists
c) 300 cars
d) 180 cars

#91. "The Best Friend of Charleston" was the first locomotive in the U.S.A. to:
a) have a boiler explosion
b) derail
c) top 100 miles per hour
d) crash into another locomotive

#92. Johnny Cash had two train-themed hits with "Folsom Prison Blues" and:
a) This Train
b) Train of Love
c) All Aboard
d) All Night Train

#93. Casey Jones, an American folklore hero, died on his train, but he did this in the end:
a) separated from the other train cars
b) put out a lethal fire
c) slowed the train to save the passengers
d) saved the passengers from train robbers

#94. In 1987, the Cuban railroad celebrated this anniversary:
a) 175 years
b) 150 years
c) 100 years
d) 125 years

#95. The windowed box on the caboose roof is called the:
a) clearstory
b) cupola
c) terrarium
d) footplate

#96. "Super Chief", a train running from Los Angeles to Chicago in the 1930s, was nicknamed:
a) Hollywood Twinkle
b) Railroad Star
c) Train of the Stars
d) Bright Lights

#97. By the age of 17, this train robber had already suffered two near-death chest wounds:
a) "Bloody Bill" Anderson
b) Jesse James
c) Cole Younger
d) Brian Field

#98. Who was the first American President to use diesel locomotives instead of steam AND the first to use an airplane for official Presidential business:
a) Dwight Eisenhower
b) Woodrow Wilson
c) Ronald Reagan
d) Franklin Roosevelt

#99. How many passenger platforms will you find at Grand Central Station?
a) 54
b) 37
c) 44
d) 59

#100. What railway operates at the highest altitude in the world?
a) Jungfrau Railway
b) Venezuela National Railways
c) Qinghai-Tibet Railway
d) Peruvian Central Railway

#101. By 1930, this happened to train robberies:
a) the criminals were sentenced to death
b) they were at an all-time record high number
c) they happened daily
d) they pretty much disappeared

#102. What is now obsolete on a train?
a) brakes
b) signals
c) engine
d) caboose

#103. Before dining cars, trains in the U.S.A. did this:
a) allowed you to pack your own food
b) the Engineer's wife cooked for the passengers
c) nobody would eat on the train
d) stopped at restaurants along the route

#104. Sheena Easton sang about a morning train in this song in 1980:
a) Early Train
b) Party Train
c) 9-5
d) Fast Train

#105. The Klondike Gold Rush was the reason for this railroad to be built:
a) White Pass and Yukon Railroad
b) Alaska Railroad
c) Great White Northern Railroad
d) Canadian National Railroad

#106. This train type holds the world speed record:
a) diesel
b) electric
c) natural gas
d) Maglev

#107. Railroads in the eastern United States were developed earlier than in the west because of:
a) lack of investors
b) Civil war
c) gold rush
d) difficult terrain

#108. Globally, signal systems are used to communicate the train route and:
a) direction
b) time
c) speed
d) turns

#109. In Australia, the train named The Ghan is short for:
a) The Ghanzalas
b) Great Honorable Australian National
c) The Afghan Express
d) The Ghanoush

#110. How much freight cargo worldwide is transported by trains?
a) 40%
b) 25%
c) 70%
d) 55%

#111. Canada's first railroad, The Grand Truck, was also:
a) underground
b) international
c) elevated
d) bilingual

#112. What was the name of the train Casey Jones drove?
a) Afternoon Flyer
b) Memphis Express
c) The Cannonball Express
d) The California Limited

#113. The Channel Tunnel, "Chunnel", built under the sea to connect England and France, was finally completed and officially opened in:
a) 1989
b) 1961
c) 1972
d) 1994

#114. Maglev trains are only in working commercial operation in these two countries:
a) Germany & China
b) Japan & China
c) England & U.S.A.
d) Germany & Japan

#115. Rail construction methods changed after Germany did this in 1924:
a) built stone bridges
b) built wider tunnels
c) created continuous welded rail
d) began using steel for rails

#116. What is the longest train tunnel in the world?
a) Gotthard Base Tunnel, Switzerland
b) Channel Tunnel, France
c) Eisenhower Tunnel, U.S.A.
d) Guoliang Tunnel, China

#117. This percentage of all English travel either begins or ends in the city of London:
a) 70%
b) 65%
c) 85%
d) 55%

#118. This 2007 film is a remake of the 1957 original film:
a) The Train
b) 3:10 to Yuma
c) The Fugitive
d) Silver Streak

#119. Classification lights on a train...
a) are located on the caboose
b) help identify schedule and train order
c) are another name for headlights
d) are in common use today

#120. A poem titled "The Railway Train" was written by:
a) Virginia Woolf
b) Mary Oliver
c) Emily Dickinson
d) Maya Angelou

#121. The Orange Blossom Special was a real train with this route:
a) Chicago to Palm Beach
b) Buffalo to Tampa
c) New York to Miami
d) New York to Orlando

#122. What railway is the world's shortest, traveling 298 feet:
a) The Angel's Flight
b) Vivek Express
c) Stourbridge Town Line
d) Premier Line

#123. This country's railway history is complicated, as it wasn't an independent country when railroads were built in Europe:
a) Hungary
b) Romania
c) Austria
d) Poland

#124. Who was the first British monarch to travel by train?
a) King Edward VII
b) King George VI
c) Queen Victoria
d) Queen Elizabeth I

#125. What is NOT a part of a steam locomotive?
a) ash pan
b) fuel pump
c) smokestack
d) sand dome

#126. American song "I've Been Working on the Railroad" can be found on a 1961 album by this singer:
a) Johnny Mathis
b) Tony Bennett
c) Frank Sinatra
d) Bing Crosby

#127. Which band member of The Who is a model train enthusiast?
a) John Entwistle
b) Roger Daltrey
c) Peter Townsend
d) Keith Moon

#128. Railroads in Russia opened in 1837 for this purpose:
a) passenger travel
b) transport freight
c) haul coal from mines
d) to connect Royal residences

#129. What type of train is mentioned in John Prine's song "Paradise"?
a) freight train
b) passenger train
c) stock train
d) coal train

#130. What is a tank car?
a) carries military tanks
b) a recessed train car
c) carries liquids or gas
d) carries aquatic life

#131. Which famous American train enthusiast appeared in television commercials for Lionel Trains in the 1970s?
a) Gene Hackman
b) Johnny Cash
c) Bruce Springsteen
d) Gary Coleman

#132. Through jungles and mountains, the railroad in Costa Rica was ready in 1890 to transport their main export:
a) cashews
b) bananas
c) coffee
d) pineapple

#133. In 1872, Miss E.M. Sawyer became the first female American:
a) Engineer
b) Telegraph operator
c) Station Master
d) Conductor

#134. This fictional TV character did NOT have model trains:
a) Gomez Addams (The Addams Family)
b) Steven Keaton (Family Ties)
c) Sheldon Cooper (The Big Bang Theory)
d) Howard Cunningham (Happy Days)

#135. What is a "cauldron car" designed to carry?
a) ice
b) potable liquids
c) minerals
d) coal

#136. This rock star has five-foot tall skyscrapers in one of his posh model railroads:
a) Rod Stewart
b) Mick Jagger
c) Don Henley
d) Billy Joel

#137. This 1995 film is about a train robbery committed by an ex-transit cop:
a) The Great Train Robbery
b) Money Train
c) Switchback
d) The Commuter

#138. The Panama Railroad carried this amount of gold during the first twelve years of business:
a) $750 million
b) $500 million
c) $900 million
d) $350 million

#139. This Rolling Stones song is set in a train station:
a) Love in Vain
b) Midnight Rambler
c) Waiting on a Friend
d) Street Fighting Man

#140. This key country in European train service was the first in the world to be largely state-owned:
a) England
b) Belgium
c) Germany
d) Hungary

#141. The peak of construction of the Trans-Siberian Railway in the 1890s had a workforce of this many people:
a) 60, 000
b) 80, 000
c) 40, 000
d) 20, 000

#142. You will find an upper-level, outdoor platform on this luxury train route:
a) Southern Comfort
b) The Adirondack
c) The Denali Star
d) Southwest Chief

#143. What is a rolling highway?
a) a train made to carry large trucks
b) a high-speed passenger train
c) a convoy of trains
d) slang for heavy train traffic

#144. Amtrack has recently added this service in the U.S.A.?
a) haul privately-owned train cars
b) haul commercial freight
c) haul fuel tankers
d) conduct passenger weddings

#145. A roundhouse is:
a) a name for early train stations
b) a locomotive engine part
c) a locomotive service & storage building
d) lodgings for railroad gangs

#146. The Baltimore & Ohio Railroad was the first American
railroad to do this on regular runs in 1827:
a) carry both passengers & freight
b) serve meals
c) issue train passes
d) carry mail

#147. At one time, this musician owned a part of Lionel, the
model train company:
a) Ringo Starr
b) Tommy Hunter
c) Bruce Springsteen
d) Neil Young

#148. In the song "People Get Ready" by the Impressions, the
train is going to:
a) Bethlehem
b) Jerusalem
c) Nazareth
d) Jordan

#149. Another name for continuous welded rail is:
a) uni-rails
b) ribbon rails
c) long rails
d) smooth rails

#150. This American businessman left school at the age of 11 and made his fortune in shipping & railroads:
a) John D. Rockefeller
b) Andrew Carnegie
c) Cornelius Vanderbilt
d) Henry Ford

#151. The 1940s film "Sun Valley Serenade" had a song about this fictional train:
a) The Hurricane Express
b) Chatanooga Choo Choo
c) The Polar Express
d) The Sunbelt Special

#152. This optimistic children's train-themed book was published in the 1930s by Watty Piper:
a) The Little Red Caboose
b) The Little Train
c) Harry Potter
d) The Little Engine That Could

#153. Roundhouses were often arranged around:
a) a lake
b) a handcar
c) the outskirts of town
d) a turntable

#154. What year was the first electric passenger train in Germany?
a) 1879
b) 1903
c) 1897
d) 1888

#155. Britain's first electric passenger train is still in use here today:
a) Brighton
b) Manchester
c) Dover
d) Newcastle

#156. The Blues Brothers sang this train-themed song:
a) Train in Vain
b) Midnight Train to Memphis
c) She Caught the Katy
d) Long Train Runnin'

#157. P.T. Barnum did this for Jenny Lind's 1850-1852 American tour:
a) arranged for her train tickets
b) paid for the first private train car
c) paid for a private train
d) sold concert tickets on train trips

#158. This country didn't have a set of standards or specifications for their railroads as they were mainly built & owned by foreign countries:
a) China
b) Australia
c) Belgium
d) Spain

#159. The slang term "ash cat" refers to this job title:
a) Engineer
b) Conductor
c) Brakeman
d) Fireman

#160. What is a "black hole" in railroad lingo?
a) smokestack
b) a mineshaft
c) a tunnel
d) the boiler

#161. The California Zephyr train runs this route:
a) New York to Los Angeles
b) Chicago to San Francisco
c) San Diego to Washington
d) San Jose to Chicago

#162. The General is an American silent film from 1926 starring this actor, who played a train Engineer:
a) Buster Keaton
b) Charlie Chaplin
c) Lon Chaney
d) John Barrymore

#163. In 1870, American railroads started issuing these to crew members:
a) company benefits
b) company pocket watches
c) company uniforms
d) paid meals

#164. Part of this railway still operates, although Lawrence of Arabia was behind acts of sabotage during World War I:
a) Jungfrau Railway
b) Mandovi Express
c) Hejaz Jordan Railway
d) Bernina Express

#165. What is a crossbuck?
a) type of train signal
b) type of railroad tie
c) X-shaped sign where tracks cross a road
d) a manual brake

#166. Hogger is a slang term for this railroad job title:
a) Engineer
b) Conductor
c) Brakeman
d) Fireman

#167. What year did Joshua Lionel Cowen patent his model train brand?
a) 1899
b) 1901
c) 1897
d) 1910

#168. What was the name of the steam train on the 1960s television sitcom "Petticoat Junction"?
a) Shady Rest Express
b) Hooterville Cannonball
c) Hooterville Express
d) Pixley Cannonball

#169. Building this railroad was very challenging due to altitude, permafrost and to not impede wildlife migration:
a) Canadian Pacific Railroad
b) Rhaetian Railroad
c) The Qingzang Railroad
d) The Sabah State Railroad

#170. What was the first named train in the world?
a) Mallard
b) Irish Mail
c) Royal Mail
d) Flying Scotsman

#171. The Liverpool & Manchester Railway in England was the first one of these in the world:
a) commercial passenger railway
b) elevated passenger railway
c) double-decker railway
d) commercial tank car railway

#172. Which is NOT a railroad job position?
a) fireman
b) tower operator
c) porter
d) cadet

#173. In 1867, North Eastern Railway workers in Britain did this:
a) took control of the railway
b) went on strike
c) died in an explosion
d) built the first Royal train

#174. This song, written by John Hartford, talks about riding the rails:
a) Gentle on My Mind
b) Morning Bugle
c) A Simple Thing as Love
d) I Walk the Line

#175. In 1838, the Great Western Railway started using:
a) electric lights
b) flushing toilets
c) air brakes
d) the telegraph

#176. What is a "ball of fire" in railroad lingo?
a) the boiler
b) a fast run
c) an Engineer with a good record
d) feeding the firebox

#177. This is one of Boxcar Willie's songs:
a) Hobo Heaven
b) Train Ride Home
c) Homebound Train
d) Casey Jones

#178. What does it mean for a train to "bake a cake"?
a) reach the top of a hill
b) build up steam
c) be at full capacity
d) ready for departure

#179. This famous train enthusiast was also the first narrator for Thomas the Tank Engine:
a) Eric Clapton
b) Ringo Starr
c) Elton John
d) Tom Hanks

#180. This train enthusiast was the creator of Thomas the Tank Engine:
a) Dr. Seuss
b) Robert Munsch
c) Reverend W. Awdry
d) Walt Disney

#181. This rail line was the most heavily used for freight until 1914:
a) Union Pacific Railroad
b) Canadian Pacific Railway
c) Panama Railway
d) Trans-Siberian Railway

#182. Currently, turntables are:
a) used globally
b) obsolete
c) used only in Europe
d) used only in Australia

#183. This singer-songwriter wrote The Canadian Railroad Trilogy:
a) Gordon Lightfoot
b) Randy Bachman
c) Murray McLauchlan
d) Bruce Cockburn

#184. The first mail moved on a train in Great Britain in this year:
a) 1910
b) 1875
c) 1850
d) 1830

#185. This 1960s Christmas song by Roger Miller is sometimes called "Little Toy Trains":
a) Christmas Toy Trains
b) Old Toy Trains
c) The Little Boy's Trains
d) Toys and Trains

#186. The high -speed train system that connects major cities in Germany is called:
a) The Bullet
b) The Link
c) The ICE
d) The LUX

#187. Which American city was a major stop of the Wabash Cannon Ball train?
a) Denver, Colorado
b) St. Louis, Missouri
c) Omaha, Nebraska
d) Tulsa, Oklahoma

#188. The Bergen Railway train in this country goes through 200 tunnels in 300 miles:
a) Norway
b) Finland
c) Scotland
d) Switzerland

#189. Kenny Rogers sings about being on a train in this song:
a) Lady
b) Lucille
c) The Gambler
d) Coward of the County

#190. "The City of New Orleans" had this in the U.S.A. in 1947:
a) the longest daylight run
b) first all-night run
c) first dining cars
d) international runs

#191. One of these does NOT help overcome the obstacle of altitude/height on a railroad:
a) funicular railroad
b) suspension bridge
c) spiral loop
d) switchback

#192. This musician was inspired to write the song Marrakesh Express after a train trip he took from Casablanca to Marrakesh:
a) Stephen Stills
b) Graham Nash
c) David Crosby
d) Allan Clarke

#193. The Burma Railway between Thailand and Burma is also known as:
a) Death Railway
b) Skeleton Railway
c) Hell's Railway
d) The Dark Railway

#194. A train trip on the Trans-Siberian route from Moscow to Vladivostock crosses this many time zones:
a) eleven
b) seven
c) nine
d) thirteen

#195. The Mount Washington Cog Railroad uses this for getting up the steep incline:
a) cable system
b) a second engine
c) rack & pinion system
d) hydraulic lift system

#196. In what country will you find the TranzAlpine train?
a) New Zealand
b) Nepal
c) Peru
d) France

#197. "The Lunatic Express" is what they call a train route connecting these two African countries:
a) Congo & Rwanda
b) Nigeria & Cameroon
c) Uganda & Kenya
d) Kenya & Ethiopia

#198. Railway Post Office clerks in the early 1900s were required to sort this much mail per hour:
a) 500 pieces
b) 600 pieces
c) 200 pieces
d) 300 pieces

#199. This 2010 movie is based on true events of a runaway train carrying toxic chemicals:
a) Union Depot
b) Unstoppable
c) Streamline Express
d) Red Signals

#200. This is a slang term for a caboose:
a) barn
b) beehive
c) alley
d) cage

Train & Railroad Trivia
Answers

#1. Internationally called railways, which country calls them railroads instead?
b) the U.S.A.

#2. The term "high ball" refers to an early type of:
a) American signaling system

#3. In 1865, a funeral train carried Abraham Lincoln's body through how many American cities?
c) 180

#4. In what year was the first steam locomotive invented?
c) 1804

#5. A train trip organized by this person in 1841 was the beginning of the first travel agency...
b) Thomas Cook

#6. Robbie Robertson tells you to catch this train in his song "Somewhere Down the Crazy River"...
b) The Blue Train

#7. What train is known as crazy eights?
a) a runaway train

#8. A train trip from Portugal to Vietnam is the longest in the world, at 10, 056 miles. How long does this trip take?
a) 12 days

#9. In what country did the Great Train Robbery occur?
c) Great Britain

#10. What gang from Indiana operated mainly in the American midwest?
d) Reno Gang

#11. How much of the world's cargo is transported by train?
c) 40%

#12. This vast railway network connects much of Russia:
b) Trans-Siberian Express

#13. What board game allows you to buy & sell railroads?
c) Monopoly

#14. The Stockton & Darlington in Great Britain was the first one of these in the world:
b) public railroad

#15. What country did not have an established railroad by 1840?
a) Mongolia

#16. The song "City of New Orleans" describes a train ride from:
d) Chicago to New Orleans

#17. How long have railroads been in continuous operation in the U.S.A.?
d) almost 200 years

#18. What are the names of the first two models of Pullman cars?
a) the Pioneer & the Springfield

#19. Modern bullet trains can reach speeds of more than:
d) 300 miles per hour

#20. The 1971 song by Cat Stevens was titled:
c) Peace Train

#21. When were diesel trains introduced in the U.S.A.?
a) 1940's

#22. "20th Century Limited" was a famous express passenger train that ran between these two cities from1902 until 1967:
b) New York & Chicago

#23. The 1980 heavy metal song "Crazy Train" was released by
c) Ozzy Osbourne

#24. What year did the Reno Gang commit the first peacetime train robbery?
c) 1866

#25. What travels on the "Spanish Train" in Chris de Burgh's song?
c) souls of the dead

#26. The majority of history's train robberies occurred in this country:
b) the U.S.A.

#27. The Orient Express was the scene for a murder detective novel by this author:
d) Agatha Christie

#28. Which is not a real, luxury train name?
a) Rocky Express

#29. Who was responsible for the 1899 Wilcox Train Robbery?
c) Butch Cassidy & the Wild Bunch

#30. What color were Russian First Class trains painted?
c) blue

#31. Where would you find the train called The Flying Hamburger in the 1930s?
b) Germany

#32. Led Zeppelin sang about being on a train in this song:
d) Bring it on Home

#33. London, England built the first subterranean railroad in the world, later known as "the Underground", in this year:
d) 1863

#34. Many years after England, this city built the second subterranean railroad in the world:
a) Budapest, Hungary

#35. What was the outcome of a race between a horse and the first steam locomotive?
a) the horse won

#36. The first steam locomotive in America was imported from England. When did they build their first train?
a) later the same year

#37. This is an Alfred Hitchcock movie from 1951:
d) Strangers on a Train

#38. What number appears on the side of the fictional steam train Thomas the Tank Engine?
a) 1

#39. What year was the Great Train Robbery?
d) 1963

#40. How many miles of train tracks were laid in the U.S.A. by 1850?
c) 9000 miles

#41. The original route for this train between Paris and Istanbul (then Constantinople) operated between 1883 & 1977:
b) Orient Express

#42. What 1987 train comedy was inspired by the 1951 movie "Strangers on a Train"?
d) Throw Momma from the Train

#43. An image of the earliest known wooden tracks used for transportation in Germany goes back to this date, well before trains were invented:
d) 1350

#44. Train transportation made it possible for the U.S.A. to end this:
b) feudalism

#45. What was the first railroad line in the U.S.A.?
a) Baltimore & Ohio Railroad

#46. What is the job title of the driver of the train?
a) Engineer

#47. Who operates the horn on an American train?
a) Engineer

#48. The song "King of the Road" is about:
b) riding the rails

#49. In what country will you find the Blue Train?
c) Africa

#50. Who stole the greatest sum from an American train robbery?
d) Newton Gang

#51. The Monkees sang about the Last Train to this place:
d) Clarksville

#52. In the mid-19th century, railroads and banks were the momentum behind:
c) capitalism

#53. What is the name of the train in Harry Potter?
b) The Hogwarts Express

#54. How did most train robbers get on the train?
a) boarded like other passengers

#55. Where is Grand Central Station located?
c) New York

#56. What is railroad gauge?
c) the width between two rails

#57. 1970s Canadian band the Stampeders had a hit with the song "Monday Morning Choo Choo" as well as this train song:
b) Sweet City Woman

#58. What happened to William Huskisson at the opening of the first railroad?
c) he was fatally wounded by a train

#59. What is a berth on a train?
c) sleeping compartment

#60. Which is not a job for the Conductor in the U.S.A.?
c) operating the horn

#61. The earliest tracks used wagons to haul:
b) heavy loads from the mines

#62. Who was "the father of railroads" in America?
b) George Stephenson

#63. Gladys Knight and the Pips sang this 1970s train-themed hit:
b) Midnight Train to Georgia

#64. Where will you find a cupola?
d) caboose

#65. Railroads made it necessary to standardize this internationally:
c) time

#66. The first rails, found in Germany for a mining cart, were made from this material:
d) wood

#67. The following is not a real train-sounding musical act:
b) Railroad Jones

#68. What is the technology behind maglev trains?
c) magnetic force

#69. Which of the following is not a real train signal system:
d) chain signal

#70. In what country will you find the Glacier Express route?
a) Switzerland

#71. The year 1891 saw the first mass-marketed model train sets in this country:
c) Germany

#72. The name of the platform for the locomotive driver is:
b) Footplate

#73. This train robber was a member of the gang from the "Great Train Robbery", who got away, for a few years...
c) Buster Edwards

#74. In what country will you find 478 km of absolutely straight railway tracks, the longest stretch in the world?
c) Australia

#75. Canada's only two train robberies were committed by Bill Miner, also:
b) an American

#76. By 1916, the U.S.A. had a quarter of a million miles of railways. Approximately how many do they have today?
c) 170, 000 miles

#77. Cuba was the first Latin American country to build railroads to transport this, not for local transportation:
c) sugar

#78. The "Settebello" luxury train in Italy has these at both the front and rear of the train:
a) observation lounges

#79. Famous basketball player LeBron James appeared in this 2015 film:
c) Trainwreck

#80. This happened in 1971 to railroads in Greece:
d) became state owned

#81. In celebration of an east-west link, the Union Pacific and Central Pacific Railroads did this:
c) the last spike is gold

#82. The joining of the American east and west by rail is sometimes called the:
a) railway wedding

#83. What is the most popular engine type in use today in the U.S.A.?
b) diesel

#84. Which American President had a special armored train car made called the Ferdinand Magellan?
b) Franklin Roosevelt

#85. Railroads are responsible for the creation of this time routine:
a) 9-5

#86. The British steam locomotive "Mallard" reached a record-setting speed of 126 mph in 1938. Since then:
d) no steam engine has broken this record

#87. Which is not a real Canadian railroad?
a) Alberta Bound

#88. Sam Smith sings about this type of train:
c) Midnight Train

#89. What is the front car of a train called?
a) locomotive

#90. In the U.S.A., what is the legal limit on the length of a freight train?
b) no legal limit exists

#91. "The Best Friend of Charleston" was the first locomotive in the U.S.A. to:
a) have a boiler explosion

#92. Johnny Cash had two train-themed hits with "Folsom Prison Blues" and:
b) Train of Love

#93. Casey Jones, an American folklore hero, died on his train, but he did this in the end:
c) slowed the train to save the passengers

#94. In 1987, the Cuban railroad celebrated this anniversary:
b) 150 years

#95. The windowed box on the caboose roof is called the:
b) cupola

#96. "Super Chief", a train running from Los Angeles to Chicago in the 1930s, was nicknamed:
c) Train of the Stars

#97. By the age of 17, this train robber had already suffered two near-death chest wounds:
b) Jesse James

#98. Who was the first American President to use diesel locomotives instead of steam AND the first to use an airplane for official Presidential business:
d) Franklin Roosevelt

#99. How many passenger platforms will you find at Grand Central Station?
c) 44

#100. What railway operates at the highest altitude in the world?
c) Qinghai-Tibet Railway

#101. By 1930, this happened to train robberies:
d) they pretty much disappeared

#102. What is now obsolete on a train?
d) caboose

#103. Before dining cars, trains in the U.S.A. did this:
d) stopped at restaurants along the route

#104. Sheena Easton sang about a morning train in this song in 1980:
c) 9-5

#105. The Klondike Gold Rush was the reason for this railroad to be built:
a) White Pass and Yukon Railroad

#106. This train type holds the world speed record:
d) Maglev

#107. Railroads in the eastern United States were developed earlier than in the west because of:
b) Civil war

#108. Globally, signal systems are used to communicate the train route and:
c) speed

#109. In Australia, the train named The Ghan is short for:
c) The Afghan Express

#110. How much freight cargo worldwide is transported by trains?
a) 40%

#111. Canada's first railroad, The Grand Truck, was also:
b) international

#112. What was the name of the train Casey Jones drove?
c) The Cannonball Express

#113. The Channel Tunnel, "Chunnel", built under the sea to connect England and France, was finally completed and officially opened in:
d) 1994

#114. Maglev trains are only in working commercial operation in these two countries:
b) Japan & China

#115. Rail construction methods changed after Germany did this in 1924:
c) created continuous welded rail

#116. What is the longest train tunnel in the world?
a) Gotthard Base Tunnel, Switzerland

#117. This percentage of all English travel either begins or ends in the city of London:
a) 70%

#118. This 2007 film is a remake of the 1957 original film:
b) 3:10 to Yuma

#119. Classification lights on a train...
b) help identify schedule and train order

#120. A poem titled "The Railway Train" was written by:
c) Emily Dickinson

#121. The Orange Blossom Special was a real train with this route:
c) New York to Miami

#122. What railway is the world's shortest, traveling 298 feet:
a) The Angel's Flight

#123. This country's railway history is complicated, as it wasn't an independent country when railroads were built in Europe:
d) Poland

#124. Who was the first British monarch to travel by train?
c) Queen Victoria

· · · · · · · · · TICKET · · · · · · · · · ·

#125. What is NOT a part of a steam locomotive?
b) fuel pump

#126. American song "I've Been Working on the Railroad" can be found on a 1961 album by this singer:
d) Bing Crosby

#127. Which band member of The Who is a model train enthusiast?
b) Roger Daltrey

#128. Railroads in Russia opened in 1837 for this purpose:
d) to connect Royal residences

#129. What type of train is mentioned in John Prine's song "Paradise"?
d) coal train

#130. What is a tank car?
c) carries liquids or gas

#131. Which famous American train enthusiast appeared in television commercials for Lionel Trains in the 1970s?
b) Johnny Cash

#132. Through jungles and mountains, the railroad in Costa Rica was ready in 1890 to transport their main export:
c) coffee

#133. In 1872, Miss E.M. Sawyer became the first female American:
b) Telegraph operator

#134. This fictional TV character did NOT have model trains:
d) Howard Cunningham (Happy Days)

#135. What is a "cauldron car" designed to carry?
d) coal

#136. This rock star has five-foot tall skyscrapers in one of his posh model railroads:
a) Rod Stewart

#137. This 1995 film is about a train robbery committed by an ex-transit cop:
b) Money Train

#138. The Panama Railroad carried this amount of gold during the first twelve years of business:
a) $750 million

#139. This Rolling Stones song is set in a train station:
a) Love in Vain

#140. This key country in European train service was the first in the world to be largely state-owned:
b) Belgium

#141. The peak of construction of the Trans-Siberian Railway in the 1890s had a workforce of this many people:
b) 80, 000

#142. You will find an upper-level, outdoor platform on this luxury train route:
c) The Denali Star

#143. What is a rolling highway?
a) a train made to carry large trucks

#144. Amtrack has recently added this service in the U.S.A.?
a) haul privately-owned train cars

#145. A roundhouse is:
c) a locomotive service & storage building

#146. The Baltimore & Ohio Railroad was the first American railroad to do this on regular runs in 1827:
a) carry both passengers & freight

#147. At one time, this musician owned a part of Lionel, the model train company:
d) Neil Young

#148. In the song "People Get Ready" by the Impressions, the train is going to:
d) Jordan

#149. Another name for continuous welded rail is:
b) ribbon rails

#150. This American businessman left school at the age of 11 and made his fortune in shipping & railroads:
c) Cornelius Vanderbilt

#151. The 1940s film "Sun Valley Serenade" had a song about this fictional train:
b) Chatanooga Choo Choo

#152. This optimistic children's train-themed book was published in the 1930s by Watty Piper:
d) The Little Engine That Could

#153. Roundhouses were often arranged around:
d) a turntable

#154. What year was the first electric passenger train in Germany?
a) 1879

#155. Britain's first electric passenger train is still in use here today:
a) Brighton

#156. The Blues Brothers sang this train-themed song:
c) She Caught the Katy

#157. P.T. Barnum did this for Jenny Lind's 1850-1852 American tour:
b) paid for the first private train car

#158. This country didn't have a set of standards or specifications for their railroads as they were mainly built & owned by foreign countries:
a) China

#159. The slang term "ash cat" refers to this job title:
d) Fireman

#160. What is a "black hole" in railroad lingo?
c) a tunnel

#161. The California Zephyr train runs this route:
b) Chicago to San Francisco

#162. The General is an American silent film from 1926 starring this actor, who played a train Engineer:
a) Buster Keaton

#163. In 1870, American railroads started issuing these to crew members:
c) company uniforms

#164. Part of this railway still operates, although Lawrence of Arabia was behind acts of sabotage during World War I:
c) Hejaz Jordan Railway

#165. What is a crossbuck?
c) X-shaped sign where tracks cross a road

#166. Hogger is a slang term for this railroad job title:
a) Engineer

#167. What year did Joshua Lionel Cowen patent his model train brand?
a) 1899

#168. What was the name of the steam train on the 1960s television sitcom "Petticoat Junction"?
b) Hooterville Cannonball

#169. Building this railroad was very challenging due to altitude, permafrost and to not impede wildlife migration:
c) The Qingzang Railroad

#170. What was the first named train in the world?
b) Irish Mail

#171. The Liverpool & Manchester Railway in England was the first one of these in the world:
a) commercial passenger railway

#172. Which is NOT a railroad job position?
d) cadet

#173. In 1867, North Eastern Railway workers in Britain did this:
b) went on strike

#174. This song, written by John Hartford, talks about riding the rails:
a) Gentle on My Mind

#175. In 1838, the Great Western Railway started using:
d) the telegraph

#176. What is a "ball of fire" in railroad lingo?
b) a fast run

#177. This is one of Boxcar Willie's songs:
a) Hobo Heaven

#178. What does it mean for a train to "bake a cake"?
b) build up steam

#179. This famous train enthusiast was also the first narrator for Thomas the Tank Engine:
b) Ringo Starr

#180. This train enthusiast was the creator of Thomas the Tank Engine:
c) Reverend W. Awdry

#181. This rail line was the most heavily used for freight until 1914:
c) Panama Railway

#182. Currently, turntables are:
b) obsolete

#183. This singer-songwriter wrote The Canadian Railroad Trilogy:
a) Gordon Lightfoot

#184. The first mail moved on a train in Great Britain in this year:
d) 1830

#185. This 1960s Christmas song by Roger Miller is sometimes called "Little Toy Trains":
b) Old Toy Trains

#186. The high -speed train system that connects major cities in Germany is called:
c) The ICE

#187. Which American city was a major stop of the Wabash Cannon Ball train?
b) St. Louis, Missouri

#188. The Bergen Railway train in this country goes through 200 tunnels in 300 miles:
a) Norway

#189. Kenny Rogers sings about being on a train in this song:
c) The Gambler

#190. "The City of New Orleans" had this in the U.S.A. in 1947:
a) the longest daylight run

#191. One of these does NOT help overcome the obstacle of altitude/height on a railroad:
b) suspension bridge

#192. This musician was inspired to write the song Marrakesh Express after a train trip he took from Casablanca to Marrakesh:
b) Graham Nash

#193. The Burma Railway between Thailand and Burma is also known as:
a) Death Railway

#194. A train trip on the Trans-Siberian route from Moscow to Vladivostock crosses this many time zones:
b) seven

#195. The Mount Washington Cog Railroad uses this for getting up the steep incline:
c) rack & pinion system

#196. In what country will you find the TranzAlpine train?
a) New Zealand

#197. "The Lunatic Express" is what they call a train route connecting these two African countries:
c) Uganda & Kenya

#198. Railway Post Office clerks in the early 1900s were required to sort this much mail per hour:
b) 600 pieces

#199. This 2010 movie is based on true events of a runaway train carrying toxic chemicals:
b) Unstoppable

#200. This is a slang term for a caboose:
d) cage

Made in the USA
Middletown, DE
13 June 2022